THE YELLOW WALLPAPER

THE YELLOW WALLPAPER

ADAPTED AND DEVISED BY LAURENCE STRANGIO AND ANNIE THOROLD
FROM THE NOVELLA BY CHARLOTTE PERKINS GILMAN

CURRENCY PRESS
The performing arts publisher

CURRENT THEATRE SERIES

First published in 2019
by Currency Press Pty Ltd,
PO Box 2287, Strawberry Hills, NSW, 2012, Australia
enquiries@currency.com.au
www.currency.com.au
in association with La Mama Theatre, Melbourne

Copyright: *The Yellow Wallpaper* © Laurence Strangio & Annie Thorold, 2017, 2019.

COPYING FOR EDUCATIONAL PURPOSES

The Australian *Copyright Act 1968* (Act) allows a maximum of one chapter or 10% of this book, whichever is the greater, to be copied by any educational institution for its educational purposes provided that that educational institution (or the body that administers it) has given a remuneration notice to Copyright Agency (CA) under the Act.

For details of the CA licence for educational institutions contact CA, 11/66 Goulburn Street, Sydney, NSW, 2000; tel: within Australia 1800 066 844 toll free; outside Australia 61 2 9394 7600; fax: 61 2 9394 7601; email: info@copyright.com.au

COPYING FOR OTHER PURPOSES

Except as permitted under the Act, for example a fair dealing for the purposes of study, research, criticism or review, no part of this book may be reproduced, stored in a retrieval system, or transmitted in any form or by any means without prior written permission. All enquiries should be made to the publisher at the address above.

Any performance or public reading of *The Yellow Wallpaper* is forbidden unless a licence has been received from the authors or the authors' agent. The purchase of this book in no way gives the purchaser the right to perform the plays in public, whether by means of a staged production or a reading. All applications for public performance should be addressed to the authors c/- Currency Press.

Typeset by Dean Nottle for Currency Press.
Cover art and design by Jason Cavanagh.

Currency Press acknowledges the Traditional Owners of the Country on which we live and work. We pay our respects to all Aboriginal and Torres Strait Islander Elders, past and present.

A catalogue record for this book is available from the National Library of Australia

Contents

THE YELLOW WALLPAPER   1

Theatre Program at the end of the playtext

The Yellow Wallpaper was first produced at La Mama Courthouse Theatre, Melbourne, on 6 November 2017, as part of La Mama's Explorations Season, with the following cast:

    THE WOMAN   Annie Thorold

Director, Laurence Strangio
Set and Costume Design, Laurence Strangio and Annie Thorold
Lighting Design, Georgia Stefania Rann
Stage Manager, Meika Clarke

CHARACTER

THE WOMAN

SETTING

The late 19th century. The present.
A large heavy table in a large airy room.

A NOTE ON THE TEXT

The text is divided between THE WOMAN and the recorded voice of her journal, RECORDED WOMAN [*voiceover*].

Where text is written in **bold** it is spoken both in voiceover and by THE WOMAN—sometimes simultaneously, sometimes as an echo—with a different attitude.

Italics denote emphasis as indicated in the original novella.

Indented lines in *italics* and square brackets [ ] indicate original text that has become action only.

The playtext follows spelling and grammatical conventions of the original novella.

A NOTE ON THE PHYSICAL PERFORMANCE

The physical language of this adaptation is as important as the text. The actions of the performer do not conform naturalistically with the descriptions within the spoken text.

Stage directions at the start of each scene indicate initial physical actions or states but not necessarily how they develop.

This playtext went to press before the end of rehearsals and may differ from the play as performed.

SCENE ONE

Music. THE WOMAN *enters slowly.*

RECORDED WOMAN: [*voiceover*] It is very seldom that mere ordinary people like John and myself secure ancestral halls for the summer.

A colonial mansion, a hereditary estate, I would say a haunted house—but that would be asking too much!

Still I will proudly declare that there is something queer about it.

Else, why should it have stood so long untenanted?

John laughs at me, of course, but one expects that in marriage.

John is practical in the extreme. He has no patience with superstition, and he scoffs openly at any talk of things not to be felt and seen and put down in figures.

John is a physician, and *perhaps—perhaps* that is one reason I do not get well faster.

You see he does not believe I am sick!

And what can one do?

If a physician of high standing, and one's own husband, assures friends and relatives that there is really nothing the matter with one but temporary nervous depression— [THE WOMAN *joins in*] **a slight hysterical tendency**—what is one to do?

My brother is also a physician, and he says the same.

So I take phosphates or phosphites—whichever it is—and tonics, and journeys, and air, and exercise, and am absolutely forbidden to 'work' until I am well again.

Personally, I disagree with their ideas.

Personally, I believe that congenial work, with excitement and change, would do me good.

But what is one to do?

I did write for a while in spite of them; but it does exhaust me a good deal—having to be so sly about it.

I sometimes fancy that in my condition if I had less opposition and more society and stimulus— But John says the very worst thing I can do is to think about my condition.

So I will let it alone and talk about the house.

The most beautiful place! It is quite alone, some three miles from the village. There is a *delicious* garden!—large and shady, full of box-bordered paths, lined with grape-covered arbours.

But there is something strange about the house—

THE WOMAN: I can feel it.

RECORDED WOMAN: [*voiceover*] I even said so to John one moonlight evening, but he said what I felt was a *draught*, and shut the window.

I get unreasonably angry with John sometimes. I'm sure I never used to be so sensitive.

But John says if I feel *so*, I shall neglect proper self-control; so I take pains to control myself—before him, at least—and that makes me very tired.

I don't like our room a bit. I wanted one downstairs that opened onto the piazza and had roses all over the window!—but John would not hear of it.

He said there was only one window and not room for two beds, and no near room for him if he took another.

He is very careful and loving, and hardly lets me stir without special direction.

And so I feel basely ungrateful not to value it more.

He said we came here solely on my account, that I was to have perfect rest and all the air I could get. So we took the nursery at the top of the house.

It is a big, airy room, the whole floor nearly, with windows that look all ways, and air and sunshine galore. It was nursery first and then playroom or gymnasium; for the windows are barred for little children, and there are rings and things in the walls.

The paper is stripped off in great patches all around the head of my bed, about as far as I can reach, and in a great place on the other side of the room low down.

SCENE ONE

Music. THE WOMAN *enters slowly.*

RECORDED WOMAN: [*voiceover*] It is very seldom that mere ordinary people like John and myself secure ancestral halls for the summer.

A colonial mansion, a hereditary estate, I would say a haunted house—but that would be asking too much!

Still I will proudly declare that there is something queer about it.

Else, why should it have stood so long untenanted?

John laughs at me, of course, but one expects that in marriage.

John is practical in the extreme. He has no patience with superstition, and he scoffs openly at any talk of things not to be felt and seen and put down in figures.

John is a physician, and *perhaps—perhaps* that is one reason I do not get well faster.

You see he does not believe I am sick!

And what can one do?

If a physician of high standing, and one's own husband, assures friends and relatives that there is really nothing the matter with one but temporary nervous depression— [THE WOMAN *joins in*] **a slight hysterical tendency**—what is one to do?

My brother is also a physician, and he says the same.

So I take phosphates or phosphites—whichever it is—and tonics, and journeys, and air, and exercise, and am absolutely forbidden to 'work' until I am well again.

Personally, I disagree with their ideas.

Personally, I believe that congenial work, with excitement and change, would do me good.

But what is one to do?

I did write for a while in spite of them; but it does exhaust me a good deal—having to be so sly about it.

I sometimes fancy that in my condition if I had less opposition and more society and stimulus— But John says the very worst thing I can do is to think about my condition.

So I will let it alone and talk about the house.

The most beautiful place! It is quite alone, some three miles from the village. There is a *delicious* garden!—large and shady, full of box-bordered paths, lined with grape-covered arbours.

But there is something strange about the house—

THE WOMAN: I can feel it.

RECORDED WOMAN: [*voiceover*] I even said so to John one moonlight evening, but he said what I felt was a *draught*, and shut the window.

I get unreasonably angry with John sometimes. I'm sure I never used to be so sensitive.

But John says if I feel *so*, I shall neglect proper self-control; so I take pains to control myself—before him, at least—and that makes me very tired.

I don't like our room a bit. I wanted one downstairs that opened onto the piazza and had roses all over the window!—but John would not hear of it.

He said there was only one window and not room for two beds, and no near room for him if he took another.

He is very careful and loving, and hardly lets me stir without special direction.

And so I feel basely ungrateful not to value it more.

He said we came here solely on my account, that I was to have perfect rest and all the air I could get. So we took the nursery at the top of the house.

It is a big, airy room, the whole floor nearly, with windows that look all ways, and air and sunshine galore. It was nursery first and then playroom or gymnasium; for the windows are barred for little children, and there are rings and things in the walls.

The paper is stripped off in great patches all around the head of my bed, about as far as I can reach, and in a great place on the other side of the room low down.

I never saw a worse paper in my life. One of those sprawling flamboyant patterns committing every artistic sin.

When you follow the lame uncertain curves for a little distance they suddenly commit suicide—plunge off at outrageous angles, destroy themselves!

The colour is repellent, almost revolting; a smouldering unclean yellow, strangely faded by the slow-turning sunlight.

No wonder the children hated it! I should hate it myself if I—

There comes John—I must put this away.

SCENE TWO

THE WOMAN *undoes her hair and lies on the table, her arms over her face.*

RECORDED WOMAN: [*voiceover*] We have been here two weeks, and I haven't felt like writing since that first day.

I am sitting by the window now, up in this atrocious nursery, and there is nothing to hinder my writing as much as I please, save lack of strength.

John is away all day, and even some nights when his cases are serious.

I am glad my case is not serious!

But these nervous troubles are dreadfully depressing.

John does not know how much I really suffer.

And it does weigh on me so not to do my duty in any way!

It is fortunate Mary is so good with the baby. **Such a dear baby!**

And yet **I *cannot* be with him**—it makes me so nervous.

John laughs at me so about this wallpaper!

At first he meant to repaper the room, but afterwards he said that I was letting it get the better of me, and cautioned me not to give way to fancy.

He said that after the wallpaper was changed it would be the heavy bedstead, and then the barred windows, and then that gate at the head of the stairs, and so on.

'You know the place is doing you good,' he said, 'and really, dear, I don't care to renovate the house just for a three months' rental.'

'Then do let us go downstairs,' I said, **'there are such pretty rooms there.'**

Then he took me in his arms and called me a blessed little goose, and said he would go down to the cellar, if I wished.

But he is right enough, of course—and I would not be so silly as to make him uncomfortable just for a whim.

I'm really getting quite fond of the big room, all but that horrid paper.

I think sometimes that if I were only well enough to write a little, it would relieve the press of ideas and rest me.

But I find I get pretty tired when I try.

I wish I could get well faster.

But I must not think about that.

This paper looks to me as if it *knew* what a vicious influence it had!

THE WOMAN: There is a recurrent spot where the pattern lolls like a broken neck and two bulbous eyes stare at you upside down.

I get positively angry with the impertinence of it.

RECORDED WOMAN: [*voiceover*] Up and down and sideways they crawl, those absurd, unblinking eyes.

I never saw such ravages as the children have made here.

The wallpaper is torn off in spots, and it sticketh fast!—they must have had perseverance as well as hatred.

Then the floor is scratched and gouged and splintered, the plaster itself is dug out here and there, and this great heavy bedstead is fairly gnawed!

But I don't mind it a bit—**only the paper.**

There comes John's sister. Such a dear girl as she is, and so careful of me!

She is a perfect and enthusiastic housekeeper. I believe she thinks it is the writing which made me sick!

But I can write when she is out, and see her a long way off from these windows.

THE WOMAN: This wallpaper has a kind of sub-pattern in a different shade, a particularly irritating one, for you can only see it in certain lights.

But when the sun is just so—I can see a strange, provoking, formless sort of figure, that seems to skulk about behind that silly and conspicuous front design.

RECORDED WOMAN: [*voiceover*] There's sister on the stairs!

SCENE THREE

THE WOMAN *moves to a corner of the room, her head against the wall.*

RECORDED WOMAN: [*voiceover*] Well, the Fourth of July is over! The people are gone and I am tired out.

John thought it might do me good to see a little company.

Of course I didn't do a thing. But it tired me all the same.

John says if I don't pick up faster he shall send me to Dr Mitchell in the fall.

But I don't want to go there. He is just like John, and my brother—only more so!

Besides, it is such an undertaking to go so far.

I'm getting dreadfully fretful and querulous.

I cry at nothing, and cry most of the time.

Of course I don't when John is here, or anybody else, but when I am alone.

And I am alone a good deal just now.

So I walk a little in the garden, or sit on the porch under the roses, and lie down up here a good deal.

I'm getting really fond of the room in spite of the wallpaper. Perhaps *because* of the wallpaper.

It dwells in my mind so!

I lie here on this great immovable bed—**it is nailed down!**—and follow that pattern about by the hour. I start at the bottom, down in the corner over there where it has not been touched, and I determine for the thousandth time that **I *will* follow that pointless pattern** to some sort of a conclusion.

I know a little of the principle of design, and I know this thing was not arranged on any laws of radiation, **or alternation, or repetition, or symmetry—**

THE WOMAN: —or anything else.

RECORDED WOMAN: [*voiceover*] Looked at in one way each breadth stands alone, the bloated curves and flourishes go waddling up and down in isolated columns of folly.

THE WOMAN: But, on the other hand, they connect diagonally—

RECORDED WOMAN: [*voiceover*] —and the sprawling outlines run off in great slanting waves of optic horror.

THE WOMAN: The whole thing goes horizontally, too—

RECORDED WOMAN: [*voiceover*] —at least it seems so, and I exhaust myself in trying to distinguish the order of its going in that direction. **They have used a horizontal breadth for a frieze**, and that adds wonderfully to the confusion.

THE WOMAN: There is one end of the room where it is almost intact, and there I can almost fancy radiation after all—

RECORDED WOMAN: [*voiceover*] It makes me tired to follow it.

THE WOMAN: I will take a nap I guess.

SCENE FOUR

THE WOMAN *lies down by the skirting board at the side wall.*

RECORDED WOMAN: [*voiceover*] I don't know why I should write this.

I don't want to.

I don't feel able.

But I *must* say what I feel and think in some way!

But the effort is getting to be greater than the relief.

John says I mustn't lose my strength, and has me take cod liver oil and lots of tonics and things.

Dear John! He loves me very dearly, and hates to have me sick. I tried to have a real earnest reasonable talk with him the other day, and tell him how I wish he would let me go and make a visit to Cousin Henry and Julia.

But he said I wasn't able to go; and I did not make out a very good case for myself, for I was crying before I had finished.

It is getting to be a great effort for me to think straight. Just **this nervous weakness** I suppose.

And **dear John** gathered me up in his arms, and carried me upstairs and laid me on the bed, and sat by me and read till it tired my head.

He said I was his darling and his comfort and all he had, and that I must take care of myself for his sake, and keep well.

There's one comfort, the baby is well and happy, and does not have to occupy this nursery with the horrid wallpaper.

What a fortunate escape!

I never thought of it before, but it is lucky that John kept *me* here after all.

Of course I never mention it to them anymore—

THE WOMAN: —I am too wise—

RECORDED WOMAN: [*voiceover*] —but I keep watch of it all the same.

THE WOMAN: There are things in that paper that nobody knows but me—or ever will.

RECORDED WOMAN: [*voiceover*] The dim shapes get clearer every day.

THE WOMAN: It is always the same shape, like a woman stooping down and creeping about behind that pattern. I don't like it a bit—

RECORDED WOMAN: [*voiceover*] I wish John would take me away from here!

SCENE FIVE

THE WOMAN *removes her shoes, approaches the table, and kneels on top of it.*

RECORDED WOMAN: [*voiceover*] It is so hard to talk with John about my case, because he is so wise, and because he loves me so.

But I tried it last night.

THE WOMAN: It was moonlight. The moon shines in all around just as the sun does.

I hate to see it sometimes, it creeps so slowly, and always comes in by one window or another.

RECORDED WOMAN: [*voiceover*] John was asleep and I hated to waken him, so I kept still and watched the moonlight on that undulating wallpaper—

THE WOMAN: —till I felt creepy.

The faint figure behind seemed to shake the pattern, just as if she wanted to get out.

[*I got up softly and went to feel and see if the paper* did *move.*]

RECORDED WOMAN: [*voiceover*] 'What is it, little girl?' said John. 'Don't go walking about like that—you'll get cold.'

THE WOMAN: I thought it was a good time to talk, so I told him that I really was not improving here, and that I wished he would take me away.

RECORDED WOMAN: [*voiceover*] 'Why, darling!' said he. 'Our lease will be up in three weeks, and I can't see how to leave before.

'The repairs are not done at home, and I cannot possibly leave town just now. Of course if you were in any danger, I could and would, but you really are better, dear, whether you can see it or not.

'I am a doctor, dear, and I know. You are gaining flesh and colour, your appetite is better, I feel really much easier about you.'

THE WOMAN: 'I don't weigh a bit more; and my appetite may be better in the evening when you are here, but it is worse when you are away!'

RECORDED WOMAN: [*voiceover*] 'Bless her little heart!' said he with a big hug. 'She shall be as sick as she pleases!'

THE WOMAN: 'So you won't go away?'

RECORDED WOMAN: [*voiceover*] 'Why, how can I, dear? It is only three weeks more and really, dear, you are better!'

THE WOMAN: 'Better in body perhaps, but—'

RECORDED WOMAN: [*voiceover*] 'My darling,' said he, with a stern, reproachful look, 'I beg of you, for my sake and for our child's sake, as well as for your own, that you will never for one instant let that idea enter your mind!

'There is nothing so dangerous, so fascinating, to a temperament like yours. It is a false and foolish fancy. Can you not trust me as a physician when I tell you so?'

THE WOMAN: So of course I said no more on that score—

RECORDED WOMAN: [*voiceover*] —and we went to sleep before long.

THE WOMAN: He thought I was asleep first, but I wasn't, and lay there for hours trying to decide whether that front pattern and the back pattern really did move together or separately.

SCENE SIX

THE WOMAN *feels along the back wall, as if measuring it with her body/shadow.*

RECORDED WOMAN: [*voiceover*] On a pattern like this, by daylight, there is a lack of sequence, a defiance of law, that is a constant irritant to a normal mind.

You think you have mastered it, but just as you get well underway in following, it turns a back somersault and there you are. It slaps you in the face, knocks you down, and tramples upon you.

It is like a bad dream.

THE WOMAN: There is one marked peculiarity about this paper, a thing nobody seems to notice but myself, and that is that it changes as the light changes.

When the sun shoots in through the east window it changes so quickly that I never can quite believe it.

That is why I watch it always.

At night in any kind of light—in twilight, in candlelight, in lamplight, and worst of all by moonlight—it becomes bars! The outside pattern I mean, and the woman behind it is as plain as can be.

I am now quite sure it is a woman.

RECORDED WOMAN: [*voiceover*] By daylight she is subdued, quiet.

I fancy it is the pattern that keeps her so still.

THE WOMAN: It keeps me quiet by the hour.

RECORDED WOMAN: [*voiceover*] I lie down ever so much now.

John says it is good for me, and to sleep all I can.

THE WOMAN: It is a very bad habit I am convinced, for you see I don't sleep.

And that cultivates deceit, for I don't tell them I'm awake—O no!

The fact is I am getting a little afraid of John.

He seems very queer sometimes.

It strikes me occasionally—just as a scientific hypothesis—that perhaps it is the paper!

I have watched John when he did not know I was looking, and I've caught him several times *looking at the paper!*

And Jennie too. I caught Jennie with her hand on it once.

She didn't know I was in the room, and when I asked her in a quiet, a very quiet voice, what she was doing with the paper, she turned around as if she had been caught stealing!

She said that the paper stained everything it touched, that she had found yellow smooches on all my clothes and John's, and she wished we would be more careful!

Did not that sound innocent?

But I know she was studying that pattern, and I am determined that nobody shall find it out but myself!

SCENE SEVEN

THE WOMAN *moves excitedly, almost dancing around the table.*

THE WOMAN: Life is very much more exciting now than it used to be. You see, I have something more to expect, to look forward to, to watch.

John is so pleased to see me improve! He laughed a little the other day, and said I seemed to be flourishing in spite of my wallpaper.

I laughed it off too. I had no intention of telling him it was *because* of the wallpaper—he would make fun of me.

He might even want to take me away.

I don't want to leave now until I have found it out.

There is a week more, and I think that will be enough.

SCENE EIGHT

THE WOMAN *kneels on the table, removing her blouse, revealing her corset beneath.*

THE WOMAN: I'm feeling ever so much better!

I don't sleep much at night, for it is so interesting to watch developments; but I sleep a good deal in the daytime.

In the daytime it is tiresome and perplexing. There are always new shades of yellow all over it. I cannot keep count of them, though I have tried.

RECORDED WOMAN: [*voiceover*] It is the strangest yellow, that wallpaper!

It makes me think of all the yellow things I ever saw—not beautiful ones like buttercups, but old foul, bad yellow things.

But there is something else about that paper—the smell!

It creeps all over the house.

I find it hovering in the dining room, skulking in the parlour, hiding in the hall, lying in wait for me on the stairs.

It gets into my hair.

Such a peculiar odour, too! I wake up in the night and find it hanging over me.

It used to disturb me at first. **I thought seriously of burning the house**—to reach the smell.

The only thing I can think of that it is like is the *colour* of the paper!

A yellow smell.

THE WOMAN: There is a very funny mark on this wall, low down, near the mop-board. A streak that runs round the room.

It goes behind every piece of furniture, except the bed—a long, straight, even *smooch*, as if it had been rubbed over and over.

I wonder how it was done and who did it, and what they did it for. Round and round and round—round and round and round—it makes me dizzy!

SCENE NINE

THE WOMAN *gets down from the table and stands addressing the audience directly.*

THE WOMAN: I really have discovered something at last.

Through watching so much at night, when it changes so, I have finally found out.

The front pattern *does* move—and no wonder! The woman behind shakes it!

Sometimes I think there are a great many women behind, and sometimes only one, and she crawls around fast, and her crawling shakes it all over.

And she is all the time trying to climb through.

But nobody could climb through that pattern—it strangles so; I think that is why it has so many heads.

They get through, and then the pattern strangles them off and makes their eyes white!

If those heads were covered or taken off it would not be half so bad.

SCENE TEN

THE WOMAN *turns sharply, as if trying to catch something out of the corner of her eye. She then feels and creeps around the skirting board.*

THE WOMAN: I think that woman gets out in the daytime!

And I'll tell you why—privately—I've seen her!

I can see her out of every one of my windows!

RECORDED WOMAN: [*voiceover*] It is the same woman, I know, for she is always creeping, and most women do not creep by daylight.

I see her on that long road under the trees, creeping along—and when a carriage comes she hides under the blackberry vines.

I don't blame her a bit.

It must be very humiliating to be caught creeping by daylight!

THE WOMAN: I always lock the door when I creep by daylight.

RECORDED WOMAN: [*voiceover*] I can't do it at night, for I know John would suspect something at once.

I wish he would take another room!

Besides, I don't want anybody to get that woman out at night but myself.

THE WOMAN: I often wonder if I could see her out of all the windows at once. But, turn as fast as I can, I can only see out of one at one time.

And though I always see her, she *may* be able to creep faster than I can turn!

RECORDED WOMAN: [*voiceover*] I have watched her sometimes away off in the open country, creeping as fast as a cloud shadow in a high wind.

SCENE ELEVEN

THE WOMAN *moves swiftly across the room, over the table, to the other wall. As she speaks she begins to draw patterns on the wall.*

THE WOMAN: If only that top pattern could be gotten off from the under one! I mean to try it, little by little.

I have found out another funny thing, but I shan't tell it this time!

RECORDED WOMAN: [*voiceover*] It does not do to trust people too much.

THE WOMAN: There are only two more days to get this paper off, and I believe John is beginning to notice. I don't like the look in his eyes.

And I heard him ask Jennie a lot of professional questions about me. She had a very good report to give.

She said I slept a good deal in the daytime.

John knows I don't sleep very well at night, even though I'm so quiet!

He asked me all sorts of questions, too, and pretended to be very loving and kind.

As if I couldn't see through him!

Still, I don't wonder he acts so, sleeping under this paper for three months.

It only *interests* me, but I feel sure John and Jennie are secretly affected by it.

SCENE TWELVE

THE WOMAN *quickly removes her corset and throws it aside—she is wearing a bright yellow modern dress that is fully revealed later when she removes her long skirt. By the end of the scene* THE WOMAN *is running freely around the room.*

THE WOMAN: Hurrah! This is the last day, but it is enough. John stayed in town over night, and won't be back until this evening.

Jennie wanted to sleep *with* me—the sly thing!—but I told her I should undoubtedly rest better all alone.

That was clever, for really I wasn't alone a bit! As soon as it was moonlight and that poor thing began to crawl and shake the pattern, I got up and ran to help her.

I pulled and she shook, I shook and she pulled, and before morning we had peeled off yards of that paper.

And when the sun came and that awful pattern began to laugh at me, I declared I would finish it today!

Jennie looked at the wall in amazement, but I told her merrily that I did it out of pure spite at the vicious thing.

She laughed and said she wouldn't mind doing it herself.

How she betrayed herself *that* time!

But I am here, and no person touches this paper but me—not *alive*!

RECORDED WOMAN: [*voiceover*] She tried to get me out of the room—it was too obvious! But I said it was so quiet and empty now that I believed I would lie down again and sleep all I could; and not to wake me even for dinner.

So now she is gone, and the servants are gone, and the furniture is gone, and there is nothing left but that great bedstead nailed down.

THE WOMAN: I quite enjoy the room, now it is bare again.

But I must get to work.

I have locked the door and thrown the key down onto the front path.

I don't want to go out, and I don't want anybody to come in, till John comes.

I want to astonish him.

RECORDED WOMAN: [*voiceover*] I've got a rope up here that even Jennie did not find. If that woman does get out, and tries to get away, I can tie her!

But I forgot I could not reach far without anything to stand on!

THE WOMAN: This bed will *not* move!

RECORDED WOMAN: [*voiceover*] I got so angry I bit off a little piece at one corner—

THE WOMAN: —but it hurt my teeth.

RECORDED WOMAN: [*voiceover*] Then I peeled off all the paper I could reach standing on the floor. It sticks horribly and the pattern just enjoys it! All those strangled heads and bulbous eyes!

I am getting angry enough to do something desperate. To jump out of the window—but the bars are too strong even to try.

THE WOMAN: Besides I wouldn't do it.

RECORDED WOMAN: [*voiceover*] I know well enough that a step like that is improper and might be misconstrued.

But I am securely fastened now by my well-hidden rope—

THE WOMAN: —you don't get *me* out in the road there with all those creeping women!

RECORDED WOMAN: [*voiceover*] I wonder if they all come out of that wallpaper as I did?

THE WOMAN: I don't want to go outside. I won't.

RECORDED WOMAN: [*voiceover*] For outside you have to creep on the ground, and everything is green instead of yellow.

But here I can creep smoothly on the floor, and my shoulder just fits in that long smooch around the wall, so I cannot lose my way.

THE WOMAN: Why there's John at the door!

It is no use, young man, you can't open it!

RECORDED WOMAN: [*voiceover*] How he does call and pound!

Now he's crying for an axe.

THE WOMAN: 'John dear!—the key is down by the front steps, under a plantain leaf!'

RECORDED WOMAN: [*voiceover*] That silenced him for a few moments. Then he said, 'Open the door, my darling!'

THE WOMAN: 'I can't.—The key is down by the front door under a plantain leaf!'

[Then I said it again, several times, very gently and slowly.]

'The key is down by the front door under a plantain leaf! ... The key is down by the front door under a plantain leaf! ... The key is down—'

RECORDED WOMAN: [*voiceover*] And so he had to go and get it, and came in.

'What is the matter?— For God's sake, what are you doing!'

[I kept on creeping just the same, but I looked at him over my shoulder.]

THE WOMAN: 'I've got out at last, in spite of you and Jane. And I've pulled off most of the paper, so you can't put me back!'

Now why should that man have fainted?

But he did, and right across my path by the wall, so that I have to creep over him every time!

> *Lights fade as* THE WOMAN *continues to run around the room freely, leaping over 'the body of John'.*

THE END

presents

THE YELLOW WALLPAPER

adapted and devised by
Laurence Strangio and **Annie Thorold**
from the novella by **Charlotte Perkins Gilman**

6-17 March, 2019

THE WOMAN **Annie Thorold**

Director **Laurence Strangio**
Set and costume design **Laurence Strangio** and **Annie Thorold**
Lighting designer **Jason Crick**
Stage manager **Laura Barnes**

An earlier version of this adaptation was presented as part of La Mama Explorations at La Mama Courthouse Theatre, Melbourne on 6-8 November, 2017

CEO & Artistic Director
Liz Jones

CEO and Manager / Producer
Caitlin Dullard

Venue Manager
Hayley Fox

Front-of-House Manager
Amber Hart

Marketing and Communications
Sophia Constantine

Design and Social Media
Jen Tran

Rebuild La Mama Fundraising Manager
Tim Stitz

Learning Producer and School Publications Coordinator
Maureen Hartley

Preservation Coordinator
Fiona Wiseman

Artistic Program manager
Xanthe Beesley

Curators
Annabel Warmington (Musica); **Amanda Anastasi** (Poetica)

La Mama office is currently at:
La Mama Courthouse, 349 Drummond Street, Carlton, Vic 3053
www.lamama.com.au | info@lamama.com.au
facebook.com/lamama.theatre | twitter.com/lamamatheatre
Office phone 03 9347 6948 | Office Mon–Fri, 10:30am–5:30pm

FRONT OF HOUSE STAFF

Alex Woollatt, Amber Hart, Anna Ellis, Annabel Warmington, Annie Thorold, Caitlin Dullard, Carmelina Di Guglielmo, Darren Vizer, Dennis Coard, Isabel Knight, Laurence Strangio, Maureen Hartley, Robyn Clancy, Sophia Constantine, Susan Bamford-Caleo and Zac Kapesis.

COMMITTEE OF MANAGEMENT

Richard Watts, Dur-é Dara, Ben Grant, Caitlin Dullard, Caroline Lee, David Levin, Helen Hopkins, Sue Broadway, Beng Oh and Liz Jones.

Our sincerest thanks to the many volunteers who generously give their time in support of La Mama.

La Mama's Committee of Management, staff and its wider theatrical community acknowledge that our theatre is on traditional Wurundjeri land.

The La Mama community acknowledges the considerable support it has received in the past decade from Jeanne Pratt and The Pratt Foundation.

La Mama is financially assisted by the Australian Government through the Australia Council—its arts funding and advisory body, the Victorian Government through Creative Victoria—Department of Premier and Cabinet, and the City of Melbourne through the Arts and Culture triennial funding program.

ACKNOWLEDGEMENTS

This project would never have begun if not for John Flaus and his partner Natalie sending me a beautiful slim volume of *The Yellow Wallpaper* many years ago and proposing the challenge to dramatise it someday.

This incarnation of *The Yellow Wallpaper* might never have happened but for an unexpected call from Caitlin Dullard in 2017 regarding La Mama Explorations. We wish to acknowledge all the staff at La Mama Theatre for their invaluable assistance; to Liz Jones and Caitlin Dullard in particular for their never-ending patience with and enthusiasm for the projects that we propose; and especially to Maureen Hartley for her constant guidance and support as La Mama Learning Producer.

To the VCAA for programming this work on the 2019 VCE Drama Playlist.

To Jason Cavanagh for creating the living artwork that became the cover design for this publication.

To Georgia Rann for entering into this spontaneous little Explorations project in 2017 and expanding its vision, up and out; and to Jason Crick for taking that spark and fanning it into flame.

And particularly to Annie Thorold for taking up this impulsive idea and being an open and wholehearted collaborator: challenging and advancing ideas, bringing spontaneity and consideration to the process, thinking on paper and on her feet, and entering fully into the embodiment of the project. Tusen tack!

CHARLOTTE PERKINS GILMAN AND THE YELLOW WALLPAPER

'It was not intended to drive people crazy, but to save people from being driven crazy, and it worked.' – Charlotte Perkins Gilman, 'Why I Wrote *The Yellow Wallpaper*', *The Forerunner*, October 1913

Charlotte Anna Perkins (later Charlotte Perkins Stetson, then Charlotte Perkins Gilman) was a prominent American feminist, essayist, fiction writer and a lecturer on women, economics and ethics. She was born in July 1860 and along with her story *The Yellow Wallpaper*, she is best known for her pioneering study *Women and Economics* (published in 1898), an analysis of the history, sociology and political economy of the female sex, which was translated into seven languages. She separated from her first husband Walter Stetson in 1888 (a rare occurrence for the time) and eventually moved to California with her young daughter.

Charlotte Perkins Gilman wrote *The Yellow Wallpaper* over two remarkable days in 1890. It was a direct response to her own experience of being prescribed a 'rest cure' following the birth of her daughter Katharine in 1885. Today her condition at that time might be described as post-natal depression.

The diagnosis of her doctor (Dr Silas Weir Mitchell) was that 'there was nothing much the matter with me' and to 'have but two hours' intellectual life a day [and] never to touch pen, brush or pencil again, as long as I lived'. After three months of obeying these instructions Perkins Gilman (then Stetson) 'cast the noted specialist's advice to the winds and went to work again—work, the normal life of every human being; ... ultimately recovering some measure of power' (as quoted in 'Why I Wrote The Yellow Wallpaper').

Perkins Gilman's condition improved significantly once she moved away from her husband, taking her young daughter with her, first to Rhode Island and then to Pasadena. There she became involved with several feminist and reformist organisations and began a career lecturing on social reform. In 1894 she sent her daughter back east to live with the girl's father and his second wife, noting that her ex-husband 'had a right to some of [Katharine's] society' and that Katharine 'had a right to know and love her father'.

Charlotte Perkins Gilman wrote *The Yellow Wallpaper* as a cautionary tale 'with its embellishments and additions (—I never had hallucinations or objections to my mural decorations)', and sent a copy to her former physician, who never acknowledged it. Gilman writes that one Boston physician at the time protested that 'such a story ought not to be written; it was enough to drive anyone mad to read it', while 'another physican, in Kansas I think, wrote to say that it was the best description of incipient insanity he had ever seen'. The text has become a touchstone of feminist thought as well as being praised as a classic of Gothic literature.

In 1900 she married Houghton Gilman and from 1909 to 1916 she wrote and edited her own magazine *The Forerunner*, presenting material that would 'stimulate thought', 'arouse hope, courage and impatience', and 'express ideas which need a special medium'. Charlotte Perkins Gilman took her own life in 1935, having been diagnosed with incurable breast cancer, determined to end her life as she had lived it, on her own terms.

If you are seeking more information or support about depression, anxiety, post-natal depression and/or suicide—for yourself or someone you know—please visit www.beyondblue.org.au or call the Beyond Blue Support service on 1300 22 4636 or contact Lifeline on 13 11 14.

Annie Thorold in The Yellow Wallpaper *as part of La Mama Explorations Season, 2017. Photo by Joshua Braybrook.*

A NOTE ON THE ADAPTATION

'There are things in that paper that nobody knows but me, or ever will.'

The Yellow Wallpaper was created as a vehicle for the performance of ideas—a monologue that is not simply presented as a 'naturalistic' direct address to the audience but conveys its hypotheses and intentions through the full expressive body of the performer. The theatrical adaptation was conceived and developed in response to particular ideas within the text—the oppression of medical and patriarchal authority, the constraints of marital and maternal responsibility, women's desire for expression and freedom (of thought, of behaviour)—and also in response to the physical limitations of text-based approaches to monologue performance.

This adaptation was also developed as a challenge to the specific skills of the performer—blending her expertise in physical theatre with the demands of text-based performance. The intention was to create a work where the language and voice of the material spoke through the body fully as well as utilising the support of key stagecraft elements (light, sound, costume, spatial dynamic, audience relationship) to respond to the body and the text—to create a work that shifts from a 'silenced' state to a fully expressive state.

The performance text operates on two key levels—in terms of language it splits the written text between the inner voice of the woman and her embodied voice (that which we hear coming from her onstage); then it further contrasts this with the physical presence and behaviour of the woman herself—a physical 'text' that counterpoints the behaviour and ideas present in the original text.

The physical language of the adaptation was developed through a process that merges intuitive impulses to the language and ideas of the text and also bodily responses to the architecture of the space itself. This process incorporated strategies taken from Anne Bogart and Tina Landau's 'Viewpoints' as well as other formal and intuitive stimuli.

The theatrical adaptation was devised in close collaboration with the performer Annie Thorold in order to truly incorporate the body and intention of the performer into the work. These dramaturgical processes include decisions about the editing and distribution of the text between the divergent voices of the piece (internal and embodied), as well as the development of the physical score of the work which is the performance's primary method of counter-staging the male-dominated attitudes implicit within the language of the text.

APPROACH TO PERFORMANCE STYLE

The primary inspiration for this adaptation has been the merging of complex text and overt physical performance through the performer. The resulting approach has been to highlight each of those elements specifically and then to examine and push the points where they diverge and intersect.

The Yellow Wallpaper is a psychologically dense text which explores the subtle shift from reason to potential psychosis in sophisticated language and refined verbal imagery. It is divided into twelve sections that chart the rest-confinement of the unnamed woman who is central to the story during her and her husband's summer rental of an old mansion. Over the course of the twelve sections the performance moves from an initial quasi-naturalism, through a growing blend of direct address and stylised physicality to a more contemporary physically and spatially dynamic performance style.

The performance uses elements of silence, stillness, heightened physicality, split delivery of text, expressive gesture, symbolic design elements, exaggerated lighting and stylised interaction with the architectural space to examine and express the psychological development of the central character.

Annie Thorold in The Yellow Wallpaper *as part of La Mama Explorations Season, 2017. Photo by Joshua Braybrook.*

USE OF LANGUAGE AND TEXT

The performance divides the text between the inner voice of the woman and her physical 'embodied' self. In the early sections of the performance we observe the woman and hear her 'inner voice' and there is a notable disjunction between the two—the brightness and propriety of her inner voice is juxtaposed with the more questioning and troubled perspective of her present self. At first the physically present woman is virtually silent—we hear only the occasional verbalised echo of her 'inner voice' and these words and phrases betray a differing perspective on the thoughts expressed.

Gradually the performance shifts between the 'inner' voice and the woman's own 'present' voice, moving from echoes and interjections to back-and-forth dialogue to a more confident dominance by the embodied voice of the performer. This self-assured voice also shifts its attention more assertively towards the audience, addressing them with animated certainty and self-possession. The 'inner' voice, too, changes in its tone and intention, becoming a positive and reassuring confidante to the presence onstage, enabling her to take action.

USE OF SPACE AND DESIGN ELEMENTS

The performance takes place in a large virtually empty room with the single set piece being a large table. This room has specific architectural features that evoke the Gothic world of the tale—a high vaulted ceiling, curved plaster mouldings, high wooden skirting-boards, glazed side doors through which light streams obliquely. The physical performance interacts strongly with these elements, the performer creating abstract shapes and nestling into crevices.

Other design elements extend the Gothic feel, for example the lighting shifts towards more angular shapes, more extended shadows; objects mentioned in the text, such as the rope and the bed, are used in ways that are oblique to the text and take on more symbolic significance. It is our intention that the yellow wallpaper itself is only suggested, not shown.

USE OF PHYSICAL PERFORMANCE

As discussed in the Note On The Adaptation, the theatricalisation of the novella is focused very strongly on expression of the text through physical performance. The language of the text is juxtaposed with the physical incarnation of The Woman—at first her physical presence is essentially still and contained but with subtle gestural hints at discomfort and contortion.

The physical dynamics of the performance progress through prone and elongated forms—on the heavy table, against the skirting board—through more adventurous explorations of the confines and crevices of the space—under the table, in corners, within the fireplace—to a more unrestrained physical looseness—leaping onto the table, tracing patterns on the walls, running wildly around the room.

Thus the performance progresses from the controlled behaviour of a dutiful wife to the unconstrained abandon of her liberated self.

Annie Thorold in The Yellow Wallpaper as part of La Mama Explorations Season, 2017. Photo by Joshua Braybrook.

LAURENCE STRANGIO
CO-DEVISOR/ DIRECTOR

Laurence is an independent director, dramaturg, theatre-maker and stage-adaptor. Recent productions include *Duras: Desire & Destruction [The Lover + Destroy, She Said]*, *Ellida* (VCE Playlist 2018) and *Hotel Bonegilla* (all for La Mama) and *Krapp's Last Tape* (fortyfivedownstairs). He has produced over 30 works at La Mama including *Beckett: Not I* and *Eh Joe* and a remount of *alias Grace* (both for La Mama 50th Birthday Festival, 2017) as well as *L'amante anglaise*, *… waiting for Godot* (VCE Playlist 2009), *The good person of Szechwan* (VCE Playlist 2013) and *La Medea*. He has also directed for Melbourne Festival, Malthouse Theatre, Red Stitch, fortyfivedownstairs, Castlemaine State Festival and Instant Café Theatre (Kuala Lumpur). Laurence has received Green Room Awards for his direction of *Portrait of [Dora]* and *Six characters in search of an author…* (VCE Playlist 2011).

ANNIE THOROLD
CO-DEVISOR/ THE WOMAN

Annie is a Swedish actor who delights in physical theatre, devised work such as *Killjoy* (Imprint Theatre Co), as well as alternative approaches to classical texts such as *The Yellow Wallpaper*. Annie has a Bachelor of Performance, Dramatic Arts from the Australian Institute of Music in Sydney. She completed her degree playing the lead in *Anna Karenina* (2016, dir. Peta Downes) and with an internship at La Mama Theatre, Melbourne. Last year Annie played the title role in the VCE Playlist production *Ellida* (dir. Laurence Strangio, La Mama Theatre). Other 2018 productions include *Duras: The Lover + Destroy, She Said* (dir. Laurence Strangio, La Mama Theatre), the feature film *Song without words* (by Bramwell Noah) and the short films *Nature* (by Elizabeth Fermanis) and *A Song for You* (by Taysha McFarland, Toprock Productions).

JASON CRICK
LIGHTING DESIGNER

Jason stumbled into theatre while someone was looking for him and isn't leaving until he's sure they're gone. Jason has designed for theatre, dance and musicals, with highlights including *My Sister Feather* (Voice In My Hands), *Lady Example* (Slown, Smallened and Son) and the Green Room Award-nominated double bill of *21 Chump Street* and *Ordinary Days* (Pursued By Bear). He also once piloted an anglerfish, and wants you to ask him about it afterwards. Jason is a graduate of the Victorian College of the Arts, and can usually be found making mischief in or around Melbourne. He hopes to create art that reaches people emotionally and creatively, but he'll settle for your thunderous applause.

LAURA BARNES
STAGE MANAGER

Laura began taking part in backstage work at the age of 15 and has hardly moved from stage left since. Working predominately in independent theatre, her recent stage management credits include *Krapp's Last Tape* (fortyfive downstairs), *Hell's Canyon* (La Mama & Old 505 Sydney), *Hotel Bonegilla*, *Survival*, *Ellida*, *Windows*, & *La Nonna* (La Mama) and *Feed* (Ringtail Theatre). She also enjoys an occasional stint in events, and recently completed a production-based internship with Midsumma Festival.

STANDING OVATION FOR
AUSTRALIA'S HOME OF INDEPENDENT THEATRE

In 2019 La Mama will celebrate 52 years of nurturing new Australian theatre.

Built in 1883 for Anthony Reuben Ford, a Carlton printer, the building in Faraday Street had been used as a workshop, a boot and shoe factory, an electrical engineering workshop and a silk underwear factory before becoming a theatre in 1967. It was established by Betty Burstall and modelled on experimental theatre activities in New York. Jack Hibberd's play *Three Old Friends* was the first play performed in the tiny space. Since that time the crowded intimacy of La Mama has provided welcome opportunities to a host of playwrights, actors, directors, technicians, filmmakers, poets and comedians, such as David Williamson, Barry Dickins, John Romeril, Tes Lyssiotis, Lloyd Jones, the Cantrills, Judith Lucy, Richard Frankland, Julia Zemiro, and Cate Blanchett... the list of those who have been nurtured there is long.

Under the capable care of Liz Jones (Artistic Director and CEO), Caitlin Dullard (Manager/Producer and Co-CEO), and a committed La Mama team, more than 50 productions are produced annually at La Mama, and at a second performance venue, the refurbished La Mama Courthouse, 349 Drummond Street, which was short-listed in May for a 2018 Victorian Australian Institute of Architects Chapter Award. An ever-increasing audience is drawn not only from the Carlton and Melbourne University environs, but from far and wide across the country.

> 'I set La Mama up, as a space for writers and directors to perform in but also it was a space where people came, as audience, to participate in the creative experiment.'
>
> —Betty Burstall, Artistic Director of La Mama 1967–76

La Mama Theatre—which on various occasions has been called headquarters, the shopfront and the birthplace of Australian Theatre—was classified by the National Trust in 1999.

> 'The two-storey brick building is of State cultural significance because it has been occupied by La Mama Theatre… The building is indelibly associated with the performance arts and is a rare manifestation of an experimental theatre in Australia…'
>
> —National Trust Classification Report

Unfortunately in May 2018 La Mama Theatre was extensively damaged by fire, caused by an electrical fault. A huge outpouring of love and support from the Carlton community, from many arts and non-arts organisations, from funding bodies, audience members, media, schools and La Mama's extensive community of artists is helping La Mama to move forward with optimism and energy.

Taking one step at a time, La Mama will continue; planning has begun and the future is bright:

> 'While there is considerable damage, this has become a restoration project. We will retain as much of the historic structure of the building as possible.
>
> We loved our building on Faraday Street, but La Mama is more than a building, and despite our devastation her spirit is strong. Together with our artists, staff and community we will move with strength into the next 50 years and beyond.'
>
> —Liz Jones and Caitlin Dullard

For updates on how you can help La Mama move on, and details of all productions and events visit: www.lamama.com.au

www.currency.com.au

Visit Currency Press' website now to:

- Buy your books online
- Browse through our full list of titles, from plays to screenplays, books on theatre, film and music, and more
- Choose a play for your school or amateur performance group by cast size and gender
- Obtain information about performance rights
- Find out about theatre productions and other performing arts news across Australia
- For students, read our study guides
- For teachers, access syllabus and other relevant information
- Sign up for our email newsletter

The performing arts publisher

A.G. (NEWMI) NEWMAN
MASK DESIGN AND CREATION

A native of London, **Newmi** took Leary's advice—tuned in, turned on and dropped out of the Philosophy program at Warwick University and set off to see the world in 1970. By 1974, he reunited in San Francisco with Furio Mariotti, an Italian leatherworker he had met in Afghanistan and apprenticed with him. Romance led him to Portland, Oregon, where he settled down, had a couple of kids, Al and Owen, studied Western saddle-making and sold leather craft in a local artisan's cooperative where he became infatuated with leather masks. In 1986, adventure called again and Newmi roamed in Hawaii and Oaxaca before settling in a bohemian enclave in the mountains bordering Oregon and California. From there he began wintering in Bali, to study mask carving, giant puppet making and shadow puppetry, taking a year off these winter sojourns to study physical theatre at Dell'Arte International (Northern California) and Leather Commedia Mask Making with Donato Sartori in Padova, Italy. Newmi has become a major global supplier of handmade leather commedia masks. He has made masks for Cirque du Soleil, The Globe Theatre in London, The Swedish National Theatre, commedia troupes and university and school theatre programs worldwide. He recently collaborated with the Make A Scene team to design and create the unique masks featured in this production of *Pinocchio*. Newmi now lives in Ubud, Bali, with his Balinese wife Juni and twin nippers Rumi and Tulsi.

HELENE FRØISLAND
COSTUME ASSISTANT

Helene is a graduate of the Bachelor of Fine Arts (Production Design) from the Victorian College of the Arts. She works as a freelance costumier and seamstress and is passionate about repurposing materials to design and create costumes. Her credits include *Festen* (Play Dead Theatre /Melbourne Theatre Company), *Three Blind Mice* (Melbourne Fringe and Adelaide Fringe), *Pieces for Small Spaces* (Lucy Guerin Inc) and *DanceON 360°* (VCA). Helene has worked as a costume assistant on *The Twelfth Night* (Essential Theatre), *Jack of Two Trades* (Monash Academy of Performing Arts) and most recently for *Pinocchio* (Make A Scene).

FELIX WATSON
SOUND COMPOSER

Felix graduated from the Bachelor of Fine Arts (Contemporary Music) from the Victorian College of the Arts in 2014. Since then he has gone on to perform around Australia and the world as a freelance trumpet player. As an emerging film and television composer, Felix has composed the scores to *The Bureau of Magical Things* (Nickelodeon/ZDF) and *Crikey! It's the Irwins* (Animal Planet/ DA's Office) as well as the film *Sleepless* (Mark Kobakian) and the video game *Henry Mosse and the Wormhole Conspiracy* (Badgoat Studios). He is currently writing a suite for a large ensemble inspired by Benjamin Britten and has aspirations to build a small boat.

JASPER FOLEY
PERFORMER AND COLLABORATOR

Jasper began his performance career in circus, studying at the National Institute of Circus Arts. He followed this with a Bachelor of Fine Arts: Acting at QUT in Brisbane. Since graduating he has performed consistently in theatre, television and comedy. He played Kevin Fitzpatrick in ABC's *The Doctor Blake Mysteries*, and performs in the sell-out shows *Completely Improvised Potter* and *Completely Improvised Shakespeare* with the company Soothplayers. Jasper has been involved with several improvised theatre and comedy groups, including *Original Cast: The Completely Improvised Musical*, performing all over Australia. Jasper has worked with Make A Scene since 2016 and in that time has performed in *Venice in Love* and *The Servant of Two Masters* (La Mama, VCE Playlist 2016). He also assisted in developing *Fooling in Love* and most recently *Pinocchio*, before jet-setting to France to study at École Philippe Gaulier.

ELOISE KENT
SET AND COSTUME DESIGN

Eloise is a Melbourne-based designer and graduate of the Master of Design for Performance from the Victorian College of the Arts. She has a keen interest in creating spaces that respond to and interact with the site, the performer and the spectator. She has collaborated with Make A Scene to design *The Servant of Two Masters* (La Mama, VCE Playlist 2016), *Fooling in Love* and *Pinocchio*. Other theatrical credits include *The Infirmary* (Triage Live Art Co.), *Carnival of Futures* (One step at a time like this), *Marie Antoinette* (Heartstring), *Her Father's Daughter* (Hotel Now), *Can't Be Tamed* (La Mama) *The Absence of Knowing* (La Mama), *La Comtesse Bis* (Melbourne French Theatre), *Life Without Me* (Illuminate Educate) and *The Merry Wives of Windsor* (Nothing But Roaring). Eloise has interned with the Schaubühne theatre in Berlin, and took part in the 2018 Besen Family Artist Program at the Malthouse Theatre.

ROSA CAMPAGNARO
ASSISTANT DIRECTOR, COLLABORATOR AND PRODUCER

Rosa is the founder and director of Make A Scene, which has been delivering her unique brand of theatre, performance technique, and training to schools, educators, and theatre professionals since 2004. She conducts Commedia dell'Arte workshops in schools and for theatre educators through Drama Victoria, La Mama Learning, Deakin University, The Fairfax Youth Initiative and Melbourne Theatre Company Education. As a valued and respected member of the profession, Rosa has been elected onto the Drama Victoria Committee and is also on the board of Lab Kelpie, an Australian new writing theatre company.

Rosa's physical theatre training includes Jacques Lecoq technique with Norman Taylor, Bouffon with Giovanni Fusetti, Commedia dell'Arte with Venezia InScena (Venice, Italy) and commedia master Antonio Fava. As well as gaining her teaching degree from Deakin University, Rosa also trained in Uta Hagen technique (HB Studio, New York) and with Patsy Rodenburg (Michael Howard Studios, New York). Rosa has created and directed original Commedia dell'Arte shows for Make A Scene, including *Fooling in Love* and *Venice in Love*, which tour schools nationally and continue to receive glowing testimonials.

Rosa was Production Assistant on the original Tony Award-winning musical, *Avenue Q* (The Vineyard Theatre, New York). Her performance credits include *Le Beatrici* by Stefano Benni (directed by Laurence Strangio) and a collaboration with Margherita Peluso on a grotesque bouffon satire, *The Devil Wears Pashmina and You?* (Elf Teatro, Milan, Italy). She has also directed Molière's *La Comtesse Bis* for Melbourne French Theatre. Rosa has also translated and published Goldoni's classic, *The Servant of Two Masters* (Currency Press, La Mama, VCE Playlist 2016). This show unleashed all of Rosa's experience and skills—writer/translator, director, and producer.

CHRISTIAN BAGIN
DIRECTOR AND COLLABORATOR

Christian is a graduate of the John Bolton Theatre School. He has been working with Make A Scene since 2013. He loves performing in and collaborating to create the company's commedia shows, because not only are they playful, interactive and fun, but due to the Italian component he is slowly learning the language! Christian is also an improviser, clown, and puppeteer and has co-devised many of the productions in which he has performed. He has worked with several independent theatre companies, including Make A Scene, Company13, Bunk Puppets, Spindly Figures, Lemony S, Black Hole Theatre, Jessica Wilson, Short Attention Span, and has been a regular member of Polyglot Theatre for over a decade. Christian has collaborated to create *Venice in Love* and *The Servant of Two Masters* (La Mama, VCE Playlist 2016), in which he played Truffaldino. Most recently he lent his creative and directing talents to develop Make A Scene's *Pinocchio*.

terror are appeased because they are bound within the metaphorical pages of the unreal and are left feeling satisfied and hopeful

Carlo Collodi's 19th century This episodes this story portrays, in the end Pinocchio emerges unscathed. The audiences' feelings of terror are appeased because they are bound within the metaphorical pages of the unreal and are left feeling satisfied and hopeful.

Collodi's original story paid homage to Commedia dell'Arte by including a scene with a *teatro dei burattini*, or marionette theatre. Commedia dell'Arte was at its peak of popularity in the 16th century and was performed on outdoor stages in *piazza* (town squares). Actors would devise a performance by improvising the dialogue and action around a specific scenario. The actors' gestures, movements and voices needed to be exaggerated and highly articulated to reach all who came to see the spectacle—especially if they were performing with a mask. Audience interaction was a regular feature of these performances.

Our production draws heavily on this tradition by linking characters with Commedia archetypes and masks. One actor, as the narrator, skillfully weaves this episodic drama together with traditional storytelling techniques, clowning, and Commedia conventions and features specially commissioned masks to aide the transformation.

Pinocchio is a delightful reimagining of this cautionary tale for kids and big kids too! A reminder that we may not be puppets but we should never stop learning and growing.

Above: Christian Bagin and Jasper Foley in rehearsal. Photo by Lisa Businovski.

Make A Scene is a theatre arts education company established in 2003. We greatly value theatre education and its power to broaden cultural experiences for young people and believe theatre education has an essential role in developing students' creativity and social engagement. Make A Scene aspires to maintain the rich and stylised theatrical tradition of Commedia dell'Arte whilst allowing for an evolution of the form so as to remain relevant and accessible to contemporary audiences, theatre educators and students. We tour our Commedia dell'Arte workshops and performances to schools and cultural events around Victoria and nationally and have received glowing testimonials.

CARLO COLLODI, PINOCCHIO & COMMEDIA DELL'ARTE

Carlo Collodi's 19th century fairytale about a transgressive puppet has delighted audiences across generations and has become synonymous with the puppet whose nose grows when it tells lies.

Pinocchio's birth into the world from an ordinary piece of wood is miraculous, as is our own, and like the puppet, we too are born into a world we quickly need to learn to negotiate.

Collodi's corrupt 19th century Italy may have influenced this allegorical story, which is still relevant today. Pinocchio's world is not always a nice place and he needs to become discerning. Through his adventures he learns about hard work, resilience, developing empathy and the benefits of showing love, kindness and gratitude. When he understands this, he is rewarded with his heart's deepest desire and finally becomes a real boy. A living breathing, feeling human being.

This pleasing resolution is the stuff that fairytales are made of and it is an important reminder of the power of fables to nurture our imaginations and appease our natural fears. Collodi originally wrote this story episodically for a children's magazine, *Il Giornale Per I Bambini*. The story ended brutally with Pinocchio left to die hanging in a tree. Collodi changed the ending and continued writing after protests and calls for the story to continue! Despite some of the grim episodes this story portrays, in the end Pinocchio emerges unscathed. The audiences' feelings of

ABOUT PINOCCHIO ...

It all began with an ordinary block of wood...

Welcome to the fantastical and dark world of *Pinocchio*—an epic adventure of villainy, danger and excitement told through multiple characters, masks, puppets and plenty of improvisation and hilarious audience interaction!

Make A Scene's adaptation is performed in the style of Commedia dell'Arte and is an innovative reimagining of Carlo Collodi's cautionary tale about the little wooden puppet who wants to become a real boy.

> "...a fine introduction to Commedia dell'Arte'—The Age *(for The Servant of Two Masters)*

Above: Jasper Foley as Pinocchio in rehearsal. Photo by Lisa Businovski.

room, playing with the puppets and masks, and trying different ways of telling, enacting and physicalising the scenes we liked and that we felt were important. This script was made through improvisation and play and a bit of writing and continues to evolve through each performance. In essence this script is just a snap shot and guide of what Jasper would say and do in this performance. There is a lot of room for improvising and part of the joy of this play is seeing the performer deal with the audience, going off script then coming back again.

Finally I have talked about Pinocchio as a he but our intention was always to have anyone play Pinocchio (regardless of gender). Pinocchio is a puppet, after all, with the potential to become anything.

Above: Christian Bagin, Jasper Foley and Rosa Campagnaro in rehearsal. Photo by Lisa Businovski.

ACKNOWLEDGEMENTS

Afsaneh Torabi (contribution to the script and development of the performance), Rachele Campagnaro (moral support and consultation on language and cultural); Sharon Davis (script consultation); Lyall Brooks (creative consultation); Lisa Businovski (cover image); Phil Speers (cover image design); Fred Martin and The Furlan Club (Melbourne) (rehearsal space); Christian Bagin and Alice Carter (rehearsal space); La Mama Theatre and Maureen Hartley (La Mama Learning Producer for her support and encouragement); Carlo Collodi for writing this timeless classic.

DIRECTOR'S NOTE

Pinocchio persistent puppet prepubescent punk perpetually pestered pain provides purpose.

Pinocchio is the tale of a classic bad boy anti-hero with a heart of gold. He is the other, he is a fish out of water, he is you and me trying to fit into this world to survive, and he is so many other things (there is a lot of analysis of *Pinocchio* out there). Rosa and I were attracted to the anti-hero nature of the protagonist but also because of the Italian origin of the tale, and the great imagery and magical transformations in it.

We made two decisions early on that constrained and informed the nature of our adaptation; we wanted to make a solo show in the style of Commedia dell'Arte. The solo nature of this play led us to the performer regularly interacting with puppets and the audience to convey scenes with multiple characters. The relationship of the performer to the audience is an important part of commedia anyway, so endowing audience members as the Blue Fairy, the Cat, and Candlewick was a lot of fun. The beautiful commedia masks built by Newmi Newman greatly informed the characterisation, voice and physicality of the performer. An interesting realisation for me is how similar Pinocchio is to the Arlecchino: impulsive, silly, playful and always hungry! So it was fitting that Pinocchio's mask reflected this commedia stock character. I'm sure Collodi was influenced by commedia, so this pairing for us was a great fit.

This adaptation was created by Jasper, Rosa and myself locked in a

La Mama office is currently at:
La Mama Courthouse, 349 Drummond Street, Carlton, Vic 3053
www.lamama.com.au | info@lamama.com.au
facebook.com/lamama.theatre | twitter.com/lamamatheatre
Office phone 03 9347 6948 | Office Mon–Fri, 10:30am–5:30pm

FRONT OF HOUSE STAFF

Alex Woollatt, Amber Hart, Anna Ellis, Annabel Warmington, Annie Thorold, Caitlin Dullard, Carmelina Di Guglielmo, Darren Vizer, Dennis Coard, Isabel Knight, Laurence Strangio, Maureen Hartley, Robyn Clancy, Sophia Constantine, Susan Bamford-Caleo and Zac Kapesis.

COMMITTEE OF MANAGEMENT

Richard Watts, Dur-é Dara, Ben Grant, Caitlin Dullard, Caroline Lee, David Levin, Helen Hopkins, Sue Broadway, Beng Oh and Liz Jones.

Our sincerest thanks to the many volunteers who generously give their time in support of La Mama.

La Mama's Committee of Management, staff and its wider theatrical community acknowledge that our theatre is on traditional Wurundjeri land.

The La Mama community acknowledges the considerable support it has received in the past decade from Jeanne Pratt and The Pratt Foundation.

La Mama is financially assisted by the Australian Government through the Australia Council—its arts funding and advisory body, the Victorian Government through Creative Victoria—Department of Premier and Cabinet, and the City of Melbourne through the Arts and Culture triennial funding program.

CEO & Artistic Director
Liz Jones

CEO and Manager / Producer
Caitlin Dullard

Venue Manager
Hayley Fox

Front-of-House Manager
Amber Hart

Marketing and Communications
Sophia Constantine

Design and Social Media
Jen Tran

Rebuild La Mama Fundraising Manager
Tim Stitz

Learning Producer and School Publications Coordinator
Maureen Hartley

Preservation Coordinator
Fiona Wiseman

Artistic Program manager
Xanthe Beesley

Curators
Annabel Warmington (Musica); **Amanda Anastasi** (Poetica)

and

present

PINOCCHIO

created by
Christian Bagin, Rosa Campagnaro and **Jasper Foley**
based on the story by **Carlo Collodi**

15-26 May, 2019

PERFORMER **Jasper Foley**

Director **Christian Bagin**
Assistant director **Rosa Campagnaro**
Set and costume designer **Eloise Kent**
Costume assistant **Helene Frøisland**
Sound composer **Felix Watson**
Mask designer and creator **A.G. (Newmi) Newman**

The actor removes the mask and wraps up the play as CARLO, *the narrator.*

CARLO: And Pinocchio turned into a real boy. *Un ragazzo per bene.* You'll also be pleased to know that Geppetto, the Blue Fairy and Pinocchio lived as a family, happily ever after. How do I know this, you ask? Well, let's just say, I cannot tell a lie!

THE END

NOTE p.14: At this point of his journey to find his father, Pinocchio is met by a large snake that blocks his path. He eventually gets past the snake only to stumble onto some private property where he is captured by the owner who makes him work as a guard dog. One evening Pinocchio stops thieves stealing the owner's poultry and is rewarded by regaining his freedom. He then sets off looking for the Blue Fairy but he arrives at her cottage to find that she has died. Her tombstone tells us that she died from the sorrow of being abandoned by Pinocchio, and the puppet becomes very sorry, bursting into a flood of tears. At this lowest point for Pinocchio, a pigeon appears and informs him that Geppetto is building a boat to cross the ocean to look for him. Pinocchio goes with the pigeon to continue the journey to find his father.

GEPPETTO: [*to the audience*] You know, I don't feel lonely anymore. Coming, Pinocchio.

PINOCCHIO PUPPET: I've got an idea. I've got some pepper … Here, put it under his nose.

The shark sneezes and the PINOCCHIO *masked character exits the booth through the shark's mouth.*

SCENE SIXTEEN

PINOCCHIO: So I rescued my papà and nursed him back to health. I also saw Fox and Cat, and guess what. They were walking around naked … Mangiaitis is such a terrible disease. Oh, and check it out, I got my father a new coat … he was never cold again. The last thing I had to do was patch things up with the Blue Fairy and she said to me … do you remember? Don't worry, I wrote it down.

PINOCCHIO *gives the* BLUE FAIRY *the following notes to read.*

Note 1:

BLUE FAIRY: Call me—0404 664 069.

PINOCCHIO: Stop, wrong one!

Note 2:

BLUE FAIRY: Bread, milk, wart off—

PINOCCHIO: No, not that one!

Note 3:

BLUE FAIRY: Pinocchio,
Even though sometimes the world has been unkind to you,
And even though you've done some silly things,
You have been brave and you've never given up.

You've also shown kindness and empathy to others, and for this you shall be rewarded. You are so much more than a puppet, you are a wonderful human being.

PINOCCHIO: *Grazie.* Thank you, Blue Fairy.

The audience member is returned to their seat.

[*To the audience*] Then midnight came and there was … *Il vento, le foglie, i lupi e un gufo.* And the Blue fairy blew … *un grande bacio* [a giant kiss].

and only myself to blame. I tried so hard to be good. I even went to school and I nearly became a real boy! One can only wonder what will become of me now.

PINOCCHIO sees the shark.

OMG, what is that!?

PINOCCHIO enters the puppet booth through the mouth of the shark. The actor changes the backdrop curtain to the shark's belly. The PINOCCHIO PUPPET appears inside the booth.

SCENE FIFTEEN

PINOCCHIO PUPPET: Where am I? Oh, gross, I'm in the belly of a shark. Oh, look, I'm not a donkey anymore! I gotta get out of here.

The PINOCCHIO PUPPET exits and GEPPETTO enters.

GEPPETTO: I've been here for two years and I'm never going to find my boy.

The PINOCCHIO PUPPET re-enters.

PINOCCHIO PUPPET: I've been here for two minutes and I'm never going to find my papà …

GEPPETTO: My boy, my beautiful little boy.

PINOCCHIO PUPPET: My papà, my old dandruffy papà.

They look at each other, and double-take.

GEPPETTO: Pinocchio?

PINOCCHIO PUPPET: Geppetto?

GEPPETTO: My boy!

PINOCCHIO PUPPET: My papà!

GEPPETTO: I missed you so much, *figlio mio* [my son]!

PINOCCHIO PUPPET: I missed you too, Papà. Actually a lot. More than I expected.

GEPPETTO: Let's go home.

PINOCCHIO PUPPET: Don't you want to travel the world and get rich?

GEPPETTO: No, Pinocchio, I have all the riches in the world right here.

They attempt to exit through the shark's tail.

GEPPETTO: We're never going to get through there, it's too tight.

PINOCCHIO PUPPET: Okay let's go this way. I got an idea.

So me and Candlewick waited until midnight and then in the distance we heard the tinkling of a bell and the sound of a thousand footsteps. There was a faint light growing brighter, and then we saw one hundred and sixty donkeys ... and they were all wearing Nikes! So funny. They were pulling a carriage full of children who were singing and laughing and having the best time ever. And at the front of the carriage was the coachmaster. He was jolly and plump like a round ball of butter. He had teeth that were iridescent yellow and they shone like a headlight when he smiled. The coachmaster looked at us with his big wide eyes and gestured for us to get in, but there was no room in the carriage, so I sat on a donkey and it bucked me off! Then the coachmaster leaned forward and bit its ear right off ... but it grew back, and we laughed and laughed and laughed, and the coachmaster's grin lit up the sky all the way to Toyland.

SCENE FOURTEEN

Sound cue of upbeat carnival music as PINOCCHIO *mimes playing carnival games and transforms into a donkey using mask.*

Sound cue of melancholy theme music which plays with the following voiceover.

VOICEOVER: *Che burattino stupidino* [What a stupid puppet], he could have been a real boy, but instead he became a donkey. *Un grande asino.* [A big donkey.] Pinocchio was sold to the circus where he had to perform for two years. One evening during a performance Pinocchio saw in the crowd *La Fata dei Capelli Blu.* He tried calling her 'Mamma, Mamma', but from his throat came only the sad bray of a donkey. The fairy left and Pinocchio cried. *Oh, che triste.* [How sad.] The ringmaster was a cruel man and punished the puppet. He said, 'This donkey is no good for my circus', and threw him in the ocean. Splash. *Nel mare.* [In the ocean.] Where he floated aimlessly ... *Povero* Pinocchio. [Poor Pinocchio.]

> PINOCCHIO, *as a donkey, speaks the following dialogue while transforming the set into a shark for the final scene.*

PINOCCHIO: So there I was, an ass, floating in the ocean. I lost everything, my papà, my mamma and my friends. I had only myself for company

And I was getting hungry, so I went to McDonald's and got a happy meal, but I was still sad and I wished for the only person who could make it all better. Blue Fairy?

SCENE THIRTEEN

PINOCCHIO *speaks to the audience member playing the* BLUE FAIRY.

PINOCCHIO: Miraculously the Blue Fairy found me, didn't you? She looked after me and I went to school. I was such a good boy. I had no Netflix, no Xbox and no screen time for a whole year. I got really great grades and then the Blue Fairy said—It's okay, I remember. You said, 'Pinocchio you've been such a good boy and you've been studying real hard. Tomorrow I will throw you a big party, *una grande festa,* and you shall become a real boy. *Un ragazzo per bene.* [A real boy.]' Imagine my excitement!

Beat.

[*To audience members*] Hey, you, come to my party, and you and you and you and ... Candlewick. I'm sorry about before, we're still besties, right? Come up here, Candlewick.

PINOCCHIO *invites the audience member playing* CANDLEWICK *to the stage.*

I love Candlewick, he's such great fun and he's always cracking me up. Like when I went to invite him to my party, he kept saying, 'Yeah, but come to Toyland'.

Lazzo of 'Come to Toyland'.

The actor sets up a game in which whenever PINOCCHIO *turns his back,* CANDLEWICK *must say, 'Yeah, but come to Toyland'.* PINOCCHIO *struggles to say 'no' and eventually gives in to* CANDLEWICK.

Hey, Candlewick, I've been looking for you everywhere. Blue Fairy is throwing me a party and I want you to come. She's going to make me a real boy! So see you at my party, okay?

CANDLEWICK: Yeah, but come to Toyland.

PINOCCHIO: Okay, I'll come to Toyland.

The actor returns CANDLEWICK *to their seat.*

What's that? It's the Field of Miracles! This is where I bury my money. Let's get rich!

PINOCCHIO *buries his five gold pieces while the music continues playing.*

I'm going to get a soy latte and when I come back I will have five million gold pieces!

PINOCCHIO *exits.*

SCENE TWELVE

The actor enters the booth to play a glove puppet version of FINNIUS FOX.

FINNIUS FOX: Gatto, look, I've got the five gold pieces!

The actor exits the booth as the PINOCCHIO *masked character.*

PINOCCHIO: My papà is going to be so proud of me. I'm going to buy him a new coat, *una bella giacca* [a nice coat], made of gold and silver with diamond buttons. Show me the money! Where is it? *I soldi?* [The money?]

PINOCCHIO *can't find his gold coins.*

Where are my coins? ... I want my coins!

Lazzo of 'I Want My Gold Coins'.

PINOCCHIO *cries and quickly becomes hysterical. Through the tears 'I want my coins' is repeated throughout the lazzo to the point where it becomes nonsensical.*

I want my dad. I'm going to find my papà.

In the following sequence PINOCCHIO *re-enacts the parts from Collodi's original story that involved the serpent, the snail and the pigeon. (See note on p.19)*

At the end of the sequence PINOCCHIO *rides an imaginary pigeon to the edge of a cliff where he sees his father in the ocean being swallowed by a wave.*

Papà! Oh no, watch out! [*To the audience*] I just stood there, waiting for him to come back up, but he never did.

Beat.

PINOCCHIO's *nose grows.*

At least I'll try. You're so good to me, Blue Fairy. Can I call you Mamma? Good. Mamma. I like the sound of that. Mamma, can I ask you a question? Why do bad things keep happening to me?

Is it because I keep making poor choices? Is it because I am a ... puppet? *Un burattino?* I don't want to be a puppet anymore ... I want to be a real boy.

Sound cue of a jazzy backing track as PINOCCHIO *sings.*

> I'm a carving from my head down to my toes,
> And it's hard to be a good boy when you're wearing paper clothes.
> I wish I hadn't run away so far ...
> Geppetto, how I wonder where you are?
> I wish I hadn't sold Dad's coat,
> But I keep doing stupid things.
> 'Cause I am just a puppet,
> Someone always pulls my strings.
> I wish that I was smart,
> And I wish that I was good.
> It's time to face the truth,
> I'm made of wood.

The backing track continues as PINOCCHIO *speaks:*

And the Blue Fairy said, 'You will become a real boy ... when you learn to speak the truth and have empathy for others ... when you are willing to go to school and work hard!' *Thank you for saying that*, Blue Fairy!

And even though school gives me pain all over my body ...
And even though I spend a lot of time in detention ...
And even though the thought of school makes me vomit ...

I am tired of being a puppet ... I want to be a real boy. So I'm going to find my papà and go straight to school, and nothing will stop me! *Vado a scuola!* [I'm going to school!]

Sound cue of upbeat funky music.

The actor opens another sign on the set: 'Campo dei Miracoli' [Field of Miracles].

CARLO *goes to exit.*

What, you're going to let me leave it there? I wouldn't end my story like that. Well, actually I did, but then I changed it because it wasn't *really* the end for Pinocchio. This is a story about hope and even in our darkest hour when there appears to be none, there is always a light at the end of the tunnel ... a lifeboat on the horizon ... a sentence with good punctuation ... you know what I mean.

And so it was for Pinocchio. He was left hanging there for ten days, but luckily he was left hanging near the house of *La Fata dei Capelli Blu* [The Blue Fairy]. The Blue Fairy was so nice. She was like the smell of freshly baked bread, or like walking through the forest after a light rain, she was like biting into a Ferrero Rocher. She was so beautiful ... *Mamma mia, che bella.* In fact she looked just like you!

CARLO *chooses an audience member to play the* BLUE FAIRY.

So *La Fata* saw Pinocchio outside her window, and she took pity on the silly puppet and decided to use her magic to free him. Come on, cast a spell.

Lazzo of 'Casting a Spell'.

CARLO *encourages the* BLUE FAIRY *to try different improvised 'spells'. The puppet is finally released with a big kiss from the* BLUE FAIRY.

CARLO *enters the booth.*

On the count of three, blow a big kiss. *Un grande bacio.* [A big kiss.] *Uno, due tre!* And Pinocchio was gently lowered to the ground.

The PINOCCHIO PUPPET *is released and then the actor, as the* PINOCCHIO *masked character, enters the playing space in front of the booth.*

SCENE ELEVEN

PINOCCHIO: [*to the* BLUE FAIRY] Where is my saviour? Excuse me, are you the beautiful angel that saved me from destruction? You are? *Oh, che brava!* [You're so good!] *Grazie mille.* [Thank you very much.] I promise I'll never be naughty again ...

PINOCCHIO *exits the stage area and into the booth.*

SCENE NINE

The following is played with finger puppets of PINOCCHIO, FINNIUS FOX *and* GATTO.

PINOCCHIO FINGER PUPPET: *Volpe, Gatto?* Fox, Cat? Where are you?

PINOCCHIO *sees two dark furry creatures.*

Who are you?
FINNIUS FOX FINGER PUPPET: We're the fox and the—I mean ... we're assassins. Give us your money!
GATTO FINGER PUPPET: *Si.*
PINOCCHIO FINGER PUPPET: No!
FINNIUS FOX FINGER PUPPET: Well, I guess we're going to have to do this the hard way.
GATTO FINGER PUPPET: *Si.*

The finger puppets chase and beat each other up.

The sequence ends with the PINOCCHIO WOODEN PUPPET *replacing the* PINOCCHIO FINGER PUPPET *and being hung up on a tree.*

PINOCCHIO FINGER PUPPET: I don't like hanging
FINNIUS FOX FINGER PUPPET: You'll hang there until you spit out your coins. We'll come back later.
GATTO FINGER PUPPET: *Si.*
FINNIUS FOX FINGER PUPPET: I'm going to get a massage. Do you want one too, Gatto?
GATTO FINGER PUPPET: *Si.*

FINNIUS FOX *and* GATTO FINGER PUPPET *exit.*

Sound cue of as Pinocchio theme music plays.

SCENE TEN

The actor transforms into CARLO *and enters the playing space in front of the booth.*

CARLO: *Povero, povero, povero* [Poor, poor, poor] Pinocchio. He should have listened to his papà, but he did not, and so he was left hanging there for the rest of his life. The End.

SCENE EIGHT

The actor transforms into the PINOCCHIO *mask character.*

PINOCCHIO: Did somebody say my name? *Ciao, ragazzi.* [Hello, guys.] So much has happened since I last saw you.

> PINOCCHIO *notices the missing poster.*

Che bello. What a handsome guy. He looks just like me. What does it say?

> *Lazzo of 'Pretending to Read'.*
> *The actor improvises guesses of what is written on the poster.*

I wish I could read. Oh, well. Guess what? I've been hanging out with Fox and Cat and we're really good friends now. Sorry, Candlewick, you've gone down a level in cool. Speaking of cool ...

> *During the following text the actor transforms the set into a forest using wooden tree props.*

... Fox and Cat are such cool people. Did you know they run a charity? They are definitely going to heaven! Anyway, we had dinner at the Inn of the Red Lobster and those two ate so much, it was so funny! Actually it's not really. You see, the poor guys have a terrible disease, it's called ... mangia ... mangia ... mangia-itis. That's it. Mangiaitis. Don't laugh. That's a real illness. Every day they have to eat heaps of food. *Tanto, tanto cibo* [Lots and lots of food]—*venti pizze* [twenty pizzas], *cinquanta lasagne* [fifty lasagnes] *e cento biscotti* [and one hundred biscuits]—otherwise all their fur falls off and they have to walk around naked. *Che triste.* [It's so sad.] I wasn't very hungry so I just ate a pepper, but I paid for everything because like they said, 'What are friends for?' Now they have gone ahead to the Field of Miracles and we're going to meet at midnight. *Mezzanotte!* There is something missing ... I know, midnight sounds.

> PINOCCHIO *sets up a soundscape with the audience.*

You guys over here make the sound of ... *il vento.* [the wind]. And you guys ... *le foglie* [leaves]. The rustling of the leaves. Over here, this group, you will be *i lupi* ... a pack of wolves! And finally, you ... *un gufo.* An owl.

PINOCCHIO PUPPET: Five thousand!? Show me the money!
FINNIUS FOX: Alright, off we go to the Field of Miracles.
PINOCCHIO PUPPET: You seem like a nice guy. *Che simpatico.* [So nice.]
FINNIUS FOX: The nicest. *Molto simpatico.* [Very nice.]

> *They exit as* FINNIUS FOX *guides the* PINOCCHIO PUPPET *out with a hand on his shoulder.*
>
> *Sound cue of the fox theme plays as they exit.*

SCENE SEVEN

The actor transforms the backdrop curtains to Geppetto's workshop/home.

GEPPETTO, *inside the puppet booth, sticks up a 'missing' poster.*

GEPPETTO: Where is that boy!? He never came home from school, he's been missing for days! I worry. My heart is breaking. If you see him please call this number or email geppetto@gmail.com, or my Twitter handle is @geppettohnohedidn't.
> But …
>
> *Sound cue of epic adventure music begins and accompanies* GEPPETTO'*s text below.*

> … if that doesn't work … I'm going to rescue Pinocchio myself! Johnny Depp and I will commandeer a boat and sail to Africa, Australia, and the jungles of Indonesia, and we will fight our way through hordes of bandits and I will bring him home, for family is the most important thing, and *nothing* will stop me!
> Ah, wait, I don't have my coat, I'll be too cold. *Troppo freddo.* I know …
>
> GEPPETTO *yanks at his underpants, pulls them off and puts them on his back.*

Oh, toasty. Here I come.

> GEPPETTO *slowly exits the booth.*

Pinocchio … here I come … I'll be there soon … anytime now.

FINNIUS FOX *enters the puppet booth and the* PINOCCHIO PUPPET *appears singing.* FINNIUS FOX *is behind the* PINOCCHIO PUPPET *and 'hiding' behind the tree branch.*

The actor performs both voices.

PINOCCHIO PUPPET: I got five gold pieces ...
FINNIUS FOX: He's got five gold pieces ...
PINOCCHIO PUPPET: I got ... Wait a minute. [*To the audience*] Was that tree singing?

The PINOCCHIO PUPPET *turns around and looks at* FINNIUS FOX *'hiding' behind the tree branch. He doesn't see him.*

Nah. I got five gold pieces ...
FINNIUS FOX: I got five gold pieces ...
PINOCCHIO PUPPET: You got five gold—Hang on a minute. Excuse me, Mr Tree, can you talk?

FINNIUS FOX *shakes his head behind the tree branch.*

I got five gold pieces.
FINNIUS FOX: He's got five gold pieces.
PINOCCHIO PUPPET: I'm going to buy my dad a coat.
FINNIUS FOX: Why not buy a speedboat?
PINOCCHIO PUPPET: I'm going to go to Bali.
FINNIUS FOX: The surfing will be gnarly.
PINOCCHIO PUPPET: I'm gonna have a lot of fun.
FINNIUS FOX: A lot of fun with my chum—
PINOCCHIO PUPPET: Wait a minute, who are you? ... *Aiutoooo!* [Help!]

When the PINOCCHIO PUPPET *realises what's going on he tries to get away but* FINNIUS FOX *catches him.*

FINNIUS FOX: Wait a minute, come back. I have a proposition.
PINOCCHIO PUPPET: But I'm too young to get married and I don't even know your name.
FINNIUS FOX: My name is Finnius Fox and I help young puppets get rich.
PINOCCHIO PUPPET: I'm a young puppet.
FINNIUS FOX: You are?
PINOCCHIO PUPPET: Yes.
FINNIUS FOX: Well, how would you like to turn your five gold pieces into five thousand?

and then we eat them! I mean, we *treat* them … kindly, you know. Yes, we give them shelter from the rain and the scorching sun and then we eat them! I mean, we *seat* them at our table and give them food. Yes, that's what we do. And then we tuck them into a warm bed with clean sheets and we cover them in butter and we eat them. Nothing to worry about. Now where is my associate? Gatto? Gatto, where are you?

>FINNIUS FOX *picks an audience member to play* GATTO.

Oh, there you are! What are you doing over there? Quick, come up here. You don't look your normal self today. What happened to your face?

>FINNIUS FOX *dresses* GATTO *as a cat.*

Ah, that's better. Now show me your cat walk. More catty. Where are your claws? Make some cat noises. *Bravo, Gatto!* [*To the audience*] Now the funny thing about Gatto is that all it says is '*si*'. [*To* GATTO] Go on, say it. What, cat got your tongue? Say it! Good. Normally I say something, then Gatto says … Good, you've got it, haven't you? Great!

>*Lazzo of 'Gatto Always Says "Si"'.*

>*In this lazzo the actor plays and improvises with the audience member by getting them to say 'si' [yes] to ridiculous things.*

>*Sound cue of* PINOCCHIO *chanting: 'I've got five gold pieces'.*

>FINNIUS FOX *and* GATTO *watch the imaginary puppet move across and behind the space.*

Gatto, that puppet has five gold pieces. Yummy! Five gold pieces would go a long way, wouldn't they? We need a plan. Have you got a plan, Gatto? Good, whisper it to me. *Bravo, Gatto!* You're a genius. That is the best plan I've ever heard. Quick, let's hide!

>FINNIUS FOX *grabs a tree branch to hide behind and* GATTO *is left to find a hiding place of its own.*

What are you doing, Gatto? I can still see you! Actually this is more of a solo mission… You hide over there.

>FINNIUS FOX *sends* GATTO *to sit back in the audience.*

MANGIAFUOCO: Nothing!
PINOCCHIO PUPPET: Are you crying?
MANGIAFUOCO: No!
PINOCCHIO PUPPET: It's okay for boys to cry.
MANGIAFUOCO: [*big build-up to a big sneeze*] Your father must-a love you very much to sell his only coat ... I won't-a burn you ... instead I'll burn that-a kid over there!
PINOCCHIO PUPPET: No, don't burn them ... they're studying to become a doctor. *Sono bravi.* [They're good.]
MANGIAFUOCO: [*sneezing again*] I can relate to that. I go to the doctor! Oh, Pinocchio, you're-a so wise. You remind me of me when I was a boy. Here, take-a these-a five gold pieces and buy a new coat for your papà.

MANGIAFUOCO *exits sneezing.*

PINOCCHIO PUPPET: Wow, five gold pieces! I got five gold pieces ...

The PINOCCHIO PUPPET *sings as he exits.*

The actor changes the backdrop curtains from puppet show to the outdoor scene and then transforms into CARLO.

SCENE FIVE

CARLO: So now Pinocchio has five gold pieces, that's fortunate, no? This is the solution to all his problems, right? Perhaps. But this puppet is still not satisfied, he wants more. More riches and more gold without having earned it. Without any hard work or effort. He has a choice here, he could buy his papà a new coat, go straight home and be the hero of this story. That would be the right thing to do ... But then there would be no need for a villain ...

SCENE SIX

Sound cue of the fox theme plays as the actor transforms into FINNIUS FOX.

FINNIUS FOX: Hello. I'm Finnius Fox, the friendliest of foxes. Yes, I am. Don't you believe me? Why, I run a charity, for children! What we do is we take children, we give them clothing, food and shelter,

Sound cue of puppet show music.

What's that?

The actor opens a sign on the set: 'Teatro dei Burattini' [Puppet Theatre].

Wow! A puppet theatre! Oh no … it costs fifty cents. I know … I'll sell my papà's coat and buy a ticket!

SCENE FOUR

The actor transforms onstage into MANGIAFUOCO.

MANGIAFUOCO: Okay, it's showtime!

Sound cue of a drum roll.

Ladies and-a gentleman, you are about to witness the extraordinary spectacular dancing puppets. *Per favore, un grande applauso.* [A big round of applause please.] On the count of three: *uno, due, tre!*

MANGIAFUOCO *enters the booth.*

Sound cue of puppet show music is repeated.

The actor changes the backdrop curtains to the puppet theatre.

Glove puppets representing Pulcinella and Arlecchino from the Commedia dell'Arte appear and the PINOCCHIO PUPPET *joins them, unintentionally ruining the performance.*

MANGIAFUOCO *enters inside the puppet booth holding the* PINOCCHIO PUPPET *by the leg.*

Signore e signori, mi dispiace. [Ladies and gentlemen, I am sorry.] I am-a very sorry for the interruption. And don't-a worry, I will-a refund your tickets, and to punish the puppet … I'm gonna burn him in my fire!

PINOCCHIO PUPPET: *Per favore* [Please] don't burn me, *Signor Mangiafuoco.*

MANGIAFUOCO: *E perchè?* [Why not?]

PINOCCHIO PUPPET: Because I am a very poor ignorant puppet and I sold my father's only coat.

MANGIAFUOCO: [*becoming emotional*] You what?

PINOCCHIO PUPPET: What's wrong?

GEPPETTO: Pinocchio, you have to be a good boy and take responsibility.
PINOCCHIO PUPPET: Okay, I'll take responsibility for this ...

> *The* PINOCCHIO PUPPET *kicks* GEPPETTO *who slowly sinks out of view.*
>
> GEPPETTO *comes back up struggling.*

GEPPETTO: No, no, no! Responsibility means you need to be a good boy by studying hard and going to school.
PINOCCHIO PUPPET: School? But I don't even have an iPad.
GEPPETTO: You're right ... Here ... take this coat, sell it and buy yourself a schoolbook.
PINOCCHIO PUPPET: Won't you be cold?
GEPPETTO: I'll be fine. Winter is not that long.

> *The* PINOCCHIO PUPPET *kicks* GEPPETTO *again and sinks out of view. The* PINOCCHIO PUPPET *re-emerges and changes backdrop curtains to the outdoors scene.*
>
> *The actor transforms into* PINOCCHIO *with the mask and enters the playing space in front of the booth.*

SCENE THREE

PINOCCHIO *discovers the world for the first time. Eventually he notices and interacts with the audience. Here* PINOCCHIO *chooses an audience member to become his 'best friend',* CANDLEWICK.

PINOCCHIO: Hey, guys! So good to meet you—and you and you and you!

> *He picks an audience member.*

Hey, nice shoes. *Come ti chiami?* [What's your name?] Did you say Candlewick? What a great name! Do you want to be friends? It feels so good to have friends. It's so good to be alive. I love being alive! Pity I gotta go to school. *Vado a scuola.* [I'm going to school.]

> *Lazzo of 'School Makes Me Sick'.*
>
> *In this lazzo* PINOCCHIO *reacts by retching at the idea of school.*

School sucks. I don't need to go to school. I believe in self-directed learning ... learning in the direction of fun!

GEPPETTO: *Prego.* [You're welcome.]

The block of wood farts loud and long and GEPPETTO *reacts.*

BLOCK OF WOOD: *Scusa. Mi dispiace.* [I'm sorry.] Wollemi pine are renowned for their odour!

GEPPETTO: *Mamma mia, che puzza.* [What a stink.] Wait, I've got an idea. I'm going to make a puppet—*un burattino*. It's going to entertain the people ... It will sing and dance and do somersaults ... And we will travel the world and be rich and famous! I will finally have a family and I won't be so lonely anymore. Let's get rich!

Lazzo of 'Geppetto Creating the Puppet'.

The actor makes milling, drilling and hammering sound effects in this lazzo.

GEPPETTO *reveals the puppet.*

Che bello, magnifico. [How beautiful, magnificent.] He's a chip off the old block.

PINOCCHIO PUPPET: Yeah, *old* being the operative word.

GEPPETTO: He's already talking!

PINOCCHIO PUPPET: Yeah, I'm talking, I'm good at talking and you're a stupid old man.

GEPPETTO: How rude!

PINOCCHIO PUPPET: Yeah, I'm rude, crude and a very bad dude. I'm out of here, old man.

Lazzo of 'Hide and Seek'.

This lazzo is a choreographed chase sequence with the PINOCCHIO PUPPET *and* GEPPETTO *inside the puppet booth.*

GEPPETTO: Wait, Pinocchio! ... Pinocchio, that's a good name ... Pinocchio, come back!

PINOCCHIO PUPPET: Where did that old guy go? Oh, here he comes. I love hide and seek!

GEPPETTO: Come here, Pinocchio!

PINOCCHIO PUPPET: Let go, old man.

GEPPETTO: Listen to your papà.

PINOCCHIO PUPPET: No!

GEPPETTO: *Ascolta!* [Listen!]

PINOCCHIO PUPPET: Why?!

[Hello!] Oh, you are very polite. *Che bella gente.* [What lovely people.] I'm sorry I was so grumpy. I don't often have visitors, so I forget how to behave. You see, I live here by myself and sometimes it gets lonely … That's okay. I have my tools to keep me company. I'm a carpenter and I love to make things in my workshop … But there is no-one to make things for. Maybe I can make something for you? A bookshelf? A table? A …

    GEPPETTO *notices the block of wood.*

Un pezzo di legno. [A piece of wood.] It's just an ordinary block of wood.

    The following text from the block of wood is a pre-recorded sound cue.

BLOCK OF WOOD: No I'm not … I'm not ordinary … I'm extraordinary! I'm hewn from the limbs of the Wollemi pine!

GEPPETTO: Wollemi pine?

    GEPPETTO *taps on the block of wood.*

BLOCK OF WOOD: Ouch! Don't do that!
GEPPETTO: Sorry.
BLOCK OF WOOD: I'm precious.
GEPPETTO: Yes you are.
BLOCK OF WOOD: I told you so, stupid.
GEPPETTO: I'm not stupid.
BLOCK OF WOOD: Yes you are. Stupid, stupid, stupid!
GEPPETTO: How dare you!

    GEPPETTO *strikes the wood.*

BLOCK OF WOOD: Awwwwwww! Ugh! … I'm upside down.
GEPPETTO: Sorry.

    He turns the block of wood around.

BLOCK OF WOOD: *Now* I'm upside down.
GEPPETTO: Oh.

    He turns the block of wood around again.

BLOCK OF WOOD: Just kidding, *now* I'm upside down.

    GEPPETTO *growls.*

Thank you.

SCENE ONE

Inside the puppet booth the backdrop curtains are set for Geppetto's home and workshop.

CARLO, *the narrator, addresses the audience.*

CARLO: *Buongiorno e benvenuti! Io mi chiamo Carlo.* [Hello and welcome! My name is Carlo.] Finally I have finished my story. Do you want to hear it? Okay! It is the story of Pinocchio ... Oh, you know it, do you? Yes, but do you know the *real* story? The one that is a bit dark and scary? The one about the silly boy who does idiotic things that get him into big trouble? *Va bene.* [Okay then.] The *real* story of Pinocchio starts like this: *Cera una volta* [Once upon a time] ...

Sound cue of the Pinocchio theme music plays under the following text.

Lazzo of 'Improvising the Setting'.

The following text may be adapted and improvised to reference the location of the performance on that day.

... there was a village about one hundred and forty-five miles northwest of Rome. It was surrounded by rolling hills and valleys covered in villas and vineyards. It was the home of the Renaissance and a place renowned for its art and literature. By all accounts it seemed like the most idyllic village in the world, and this village is the setting for my story, a story that begins with ... *un pezzo di legno* [a block of wood].

CARLO *takes a block of wood out of the suitcase.*

SCENE TWO

The actor transforms onstage into GEPPETTO.

GEPPETTO: Where are my tools?! I can't do any work without my tools! Did you take my tools? What have you done with my tools? *Scusa.* [I'm sorry.] I didn't mean to frighten you ... *Benvenuti a casa mia, Io sono Geppetto.* [Welcome to my home, I am Geppetto.] *Buongiorno!*

DESIGN & STAGING

The set is made up of a large puppet booth with internal backdrop curtains that change to establish locations such as Geppetto's workshop/home and the belly of a shark. There are two prop stations in front of the set, one on either side. Each comprises a vintage suitcase full of masks, props and costumes for the many character transformations the actor makes. Pre-recorded sound cues and music and voice-over are used in this production.

TRANSLATION OF ITALIAN WORDS AND PHRASES

An English translation of the Italian words and phrases is provided immediately after in square brackets. The actor may choose the Italian or English text. If they choose to say both, it is recommended as a general rule to say the Italian first.

Mangiafuoco is pronounced MAHN-jə-FWOH-koh.

A NOTE ON LAZZO

Stage directions indicate where a rehearsed *lazzo* is required and a description of the type of *lazzo* it is.

There are a few theories on the origins of the word *lazzo*. It is commonly believed that the word originates from the Italian meaning joke or jest. It could also be derived from the Italian *lazzarone* which translates to slacker or scoundrel. The word may even originate from *laccio*, which translates to string or rope, and may signify 'tying up the action'. Whatever the origins, most seem to agree that *lazzi* are physical and verbal games, jokes or gags performed by the actors on stage, often including interaction or 'play' with the audience. *Lazzi* can be silly slapstick, comic business or a variety of comic routines, rehearsed or improvised.

CHARACTERS

CARLO, narrator (unmasked character)

GEPPETTO, Pinocchio's creator and *papà* (wears Pantalone mask)

PINOCCHIO, a masked character (wears Arlecchino mask) and also played as a wooden puppet

MANGIAFUOCO, puppet master and theatre director (wears Il Capitano mask)

FINNIUS FOX, the villain (masked character)

GATTO, another villain

THE BLUE FAIRY, a mother figure to Pinocchio

CANDLEWICK, Pinocchio's mischievous best friend

One actor plays Carlo, Geppetto, Pinocchio, Mangiafuoco and Finnius Fox, switching between characters through the use of Commedia dell'Arte masks and puppets.

Gatto, The Blue Fairy and Candlewick who are played by randomly selected audience members.

SETTING

The original story by Carlo Collodi is set in 19th-century Italy.

A NOTE ON THIS TEXT

This script is a working document that reflects an ongoing creative process. It documents the production at the time of printing before it was staged for public performance. It was developed through improvisation and play and a bit of writing and continues to evolve through each performance. In essence this script is just a snapshot and guide to what the actor would say and do in performance.

Pinocchio was first presented at La Mama Courthouse, Melbourne, on 15 May, 2019, with the following cast:

    PERFORMER   Jasper Foley

Director, Christian Bagin
Assistant Director, Rosa Campagnaro
Set and Costume Designer, Eloise Kent
Costume Assistant, Helene Frøisland
Sound Composer, Felix Watson
Mask Designer and Creator, A.G. (Newmi) Newman

Contents

PINOCCHIO 1

Theatre Program at the end of the playtext

CURRENT THEATRE SERIES

First published in 2019
by Currency Press Pty Ltd,
PO Box 2287, Strawberry Hills, NSW, 2012, Australia
enquiries@currency.com.au
www.currency.com.au

in association with La Mama Theatre, Melbourne

Copyright: *Pinocchio* © Christian Bagin, Rosa Campagnaro & Jasper Foley, 2019.

COPYING FOR EDUCATIONAL PURPOSES

The Australian *Copyright Act 1968* (Act) allows a maximum of one chapter or 10% of this book, whichever is the greater, to be copied by any educational institution for its educational purposes provided that that educational institution (or the body that administers it) has given a remuneration notice to Copyright Agency (CA) under the Act.

For details of the CA licence for educational institutions contact CA, 11/66 Goulburn Street, Sydney, NSW, 2000; tel: within Australia 1800 066 844 toll free; outside Australia 61 2 9394 7600; fax: 61 2 9394 7601; email: info@copyright.com.au

COPYING FOR OTHER PURPOSES

Except as permitted under the Act, for example a fair dealing for the purposes of study, research, criticism or review, no part of this book may be reproduced, stored in a retrieval system, or transmitted in any form or by any means without prior written permission. All enquiries should be made to the publisher at the address above.

Any performance or public reading of *Pinocchio* is forbidden unless a licence has been received from the authors or the authors' agent. The purchase of this book in no way gives the purchaser the right to perform the plays in public, whether by means of a staged production or a reading. All applications for public performance should be addressed to the authors c/- Currency Press.

Typeset by Dean Nottle for Currency Press.
Printed by Fineline Print + Copy Services, St Peters, NSW.
Initial cover concept by Phil Speers, photographs by Lisa Businovski.
Cover design by Katy Wall.

A catalogue record for this book is available from the National Library of Australia

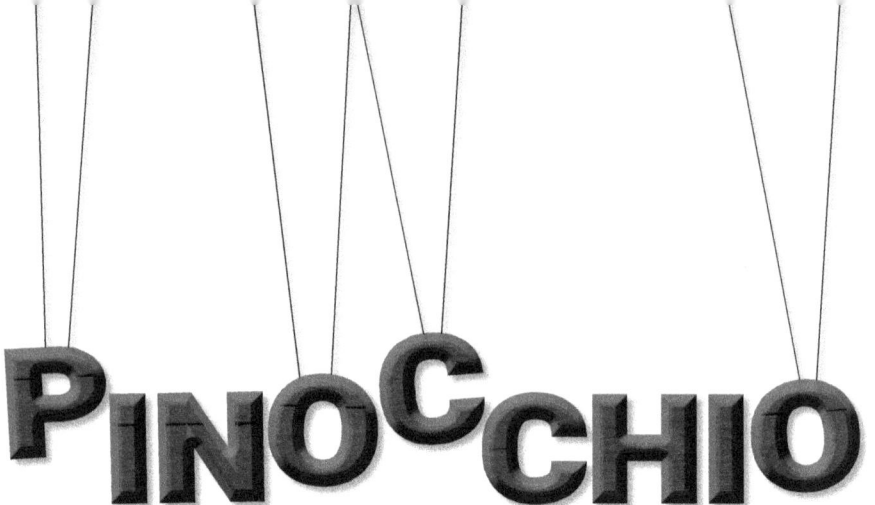

PINOCCHIO

created by
Christian Bagin, Rosa Campagnaro and Jasper Foley
based on the story by
Carlo Collodi

CURRENCY PRESS
The performing arts publisher

PINOCCHIO

www.ingramcontent.com/pod-product-compliance
Lightning Source LLC
Chambersburg PA
CBHW050021090426
42734CB00021B/3366